The General C

Burme
G000070851

by Philippe de Vosjoli

Table of Contents

Introduction

In the early 1970's the author was fortunate in obtaining a hatchling Burmese python which in time grew into an impressive twelve foot animal with an outstanding docile temperament. Of all the snakes that the author has owned, none has ever equalled this particular animal in terms of personality and responsiveness. This Burmese python eventually appeared in a number of newspaper articles, in herpetological shows and in several classroom and school presentations on amphibians and reptiles. This special animal performed innumerable services in helping to dispel myths and popular misconceptions about snakes, tolerating at times more than a dozen little hands trying to get a feel of the skin of a living giant snake.

Beauty, slow movement, heavy bodied proportions, calm disposition and a greater degree of responsiveness than demonstrated by most other snake species have made the Burmese python a favorite among those seeking to own a snake pet. Yet Burmese pythons are in several ways far from the ideal pet snake. In spite of the docile personality of many specimens (this will depend on genetics as well as frequency and quality of interaction), the fact is that Burmese pythons usually grow into large, heavy, powerful predators that have feeding, housing and handling requirements that will not make them suitable as pets for many members of the general public. Just as with certain dog breeds, Burmese pythons are not recommended for everyone.

Today with the rapid advances in herpetoculture, increasing numbers of captive-bred Burmese pythons are purchased by budding herpetoculturists as snake pets. The growing popularity of Burmese pythons is at one level an indication of a slowly growing change of attitude by the general population towards reptiles and reptile keeping. At another level the keeping of large snakes by members of the general population has become a concern of certain states, cities and townships who question the wisdom of allowing private individuals to keep what they consider "potentially dangerous" large constrictors. The result has been the numerous legislative proposals put forth to various agencies every year in an attempt to restrict herpetoculturists from keeping large snakes. Most of these proposals are based on speculation rather than fact and many, at a time when the general public should be better educated about the world they live in, indirectly perpetuate bias, misinformation, superstition and myth about these snakes.

The purpose of this book is to address some of these issues and to present facts and guidelines for the responsible keeping and breeding of Burmese pythons and other large species of pythons.

Acknowledgements
Special thanks to Bob Clark of Oklahoma City, Ok., and Ernie Wagner of Seattle WA., for their review of the material and invaluable advice.

Before Buying a Burmese Python

Many people who buy Burmese pythons probably should not. They have no clear notion of the difference between the small hatchling which can be held in one hand and be housed in a ten gallon vivarium and the large adult which may require two people for handling and will require a cage that will take up a significant portion of a room. Most first time Burmese python buyers also don't fully grasp the fact that they will start by feeding their baby snake a mouse and end up with having to feed it large rabbits..

If you want a large snake, there are other species which don't grow quite as large and are easier to handle as adults such as boa constrictors, Dumeril's boas, rainbow boas, ball pythons and carpet pythons. Granted, Burmese pythons also have great qualities: large and impressive size, beauty and many, when captive raised from juveniles, have about the nicest personality you can find in a snake. But is a giant snake really what you want?

This type of decision is no different than that which confronts a dog buyer. Before purchasing a snake, one must consider one's lifestyle such as whether one lives in an apartment or a large home, whether one has children, how much free time one has, the ease of obtaining required food items as well as the selection of the breed, say a kingsnake, rainbow boa, boa constrictor or a Burmese python. Is the Burmese python going to end up in your studio apartment or in a special room on the bottom floor of the house? Are your young children likely to tamper with it? If you're an older person, will you be able to handle it when it exceeds 60 pounds? Will there be someone there to help you? These are the things one should think about if one intends to be a responsible snake owner.

BEING A RESPONSIBLE SNAKE OWNER

Every year, hundreds of pet snakes in the U.S. escape from their inadequate cages. Many are never heard of again. Others end up making the news including many escapee large constrictors (the State of Florida seems to be # 1 on the list for reported escaped large constrictors). Every time this happens, this gives fuel to those who want to oppose the keeping of exotic animals including large constrictors by the private sector. In addition, bad P.R. is caused by individuals who take their snakes out in public places outside of the proper forum for such displays and by individuals who intentionally aim to shock people. The news media loves incidents that involve reptiles. The public subconsciously must look forward to these incidents. It gives them something to talk about and it didn't even have to come out of the National Enquirer.

RESPONSIBLE SNAKE OWNERSHIP

In terms of snake ownership, the author supports some of the views recently presented by board members of the American Federation of Herpetoculturists, a non-profit organization which represents the interests of herpetoculturists while taking into consideration both the welfare of the general public and the welfare of amphibians and reptiles. The AFH emphasizes responsible herpetoculture as the backbone of its position on the keeping of amphibians and reptiles. With regard to the ownership of large constrictors, an outline of the AFH views which has been presented at several hearings in Southern California is as follows:

A. In consideration of the right of the general public not to be exposed unexpectedly to snakes such as large constrictors and in consideration of the irresponsible behavior of certain snake owners, the AFH recommends that snakes not be openly displayed in a public setting outside of proper and established forums for such practices such as herpetological shows, educational displays, pet stores and presentations, and other special displays whereby members of the public are forewarned that a snake(s) may be displayed in the open.

B. The AFH recommends that all snakes be transported in a manner that precludes escape: In a sturdy cloth bag free of holes or tears which is then placed inside a

Adult female Burmese python

box or similar container with holes for aeration. The box or container should then be sealed or locked shut. Another alternative is to double bag snakes. Care must be taken to use sturdy cloth bags with a weave that allows for adequate air flow. Airlines should be consulted as to their requirements when shipping snakes by air.

C. For the keeping of large constrictors eight feet or more, the AFH recommends general caging regulations whose effects are similar to those which require dog owners to keep their pets within the confines of their property. Caging regulations for large snakes should require owners of such snakes to house them in secure cages with hinged top or doors or a sliding glass front which include a locking mechanism. Such enclosures should preferably be contained in a large room modified to prevent snake escapes and with a door which shall be kept shut or locked when not occupied by the owners. This recommendation is made to require responsible herpetocultural practices by individuals in consideration for the animals, for family members and for members of the general public. As herpetoculturists we will all benefit by adopting these responsible practices.

D. When handling any of the giant snakes (Green anaconda, Indian and Burmese python, African rock python, reticulated python and amethystine python) over 8 feet, the AFH recommends that another individual be present or at the very least within calling reach. The probability of any serious problem occurring when handling such snakes is very remote but the AFH position is that herpetoculturists, out of responsibility to themselves, to family members and to other herpetoculturists, should handle and maintain large snakes in a manner that significantly prevents the likelihood of any accident or incident.

E. The AFH does not recommend the ownership of the above mentioned giant constrictors as well as other large (adult size over seven feet) boid snakes by minors without parental consent to assume responsibility for proper housing, maintenance and supervision when handling.

F. As with any other animals such as dogs, owners of large constrictors should remember that they can be liable for the medical costs of treating injuries as well as additional financial damages for traumas or damage caused by their animals.

The AFH is currently drafting an official statement on the keeping of large constricting snakes by the private sector as well as a legislative package to help herpetocultural organizations contend with legislative issues relating to this matter.

For information write to: The American Federation of Herpetoculturists, P.O. Box 1131, Lakeside, CA, 92040.

WHAT ABOUT REGULATIONS?

There appears to have been a trend in the last few years for cities or states to draft ordinances or regulations to control or restrict ownership of large snakes. Various agencies or organizations directly or indirectly support these regulations particularly with regards to the ownership of large constrictors (typically boas and pythons which can achieve an adult length of over 8 feet). They contend that the public should be protected from the remote possibility of danger from these animals. Most of these proposed regulations conceal the underlying persistent bias against snakes which to this day permeates the attitudes of many people against reptiles.

One would assume from these regulations that potentially dangerous things should not, as a matter of course be possessed by the general public. One could also be led to believe that these various agencies look out for our welfare. In fact, our lives are routinely affected by much greater probabilities of danger than presented by large constrictors that are condoned by numerous agencies as well as the federal government. Dogs raised and kept by irresponsible owners are clearly dangerous as plenty of statistical data indicates (10-15 deaths per year, millions of dollars spent in treating bites). Cats can be dangerous. They can claw (many people don't seem to mind). They also account for a significant percentage of reported animal bites and can carry some nasty diseases. Living near other human beings can be very dangerous. In fact, based on available statistics, a human being has a far greater chance of being seriously injured from a bite by a fellow human than by a large constrictor.

The cars we drive are potentially dangerous as several thousand deaths every year indicate. So is ownership of guns. Horses, if one were to look at available data in the U.S., are one of the most dangerous of domestic animals and many times more dangerous than snakes in terms of deaths and accidents. The electrical appliances in our house are dangerous as is the use of natural gas. So is drinking alcohol and smoking.

In the midst of such numerous potential dangers which are an intrinsic part of life, poorly informed and biased state and local agencies regularly propose laws and ordinances which would attempt to ban ownership of large constrictors. If one relied on hard data rather than prejudice, one could make a much better case for banning ownership of dogs, horses, guns, automobiles etc.

In the case of Burmese pythons, what becomes evident is that they have an extremely low behavioral propensity to kill humans by constriction. In one report which investigated authenticated deaths by large constrictors in the U.S. between 1978 and 1988 (4 deaths were reported of which three were caused by reticulated

6

pythons), one incident involved a Burmese python. Furthermore, at least three of the cases involved irresponsible herpetoculturalpractices. Considering the many large constrictors, including tens of thousands of Burmese pythons which have been imported and sold during that period, and considering the much more threatening dangers which are generally accepted as a normal part of every day life, the potential danger presented by large constrictors pales.

With a minimum of common sense and by adopting the recommenda tions made by herpetological organizations such as the AFH, any

Hatchling Burmese python

problems associated with the ownership of large snakes can be addressed in a responsible manner without perpetuating bias and misinformation and without threatening the rights of herpetoculturists to practice their avocation.

Nonetheless....

Before purchasing a Burmese python or any other large constrictor, check your state, county and local regulations for any provisions applying to the ownership of reptiles by individuals. Besides contacting the agencies in charge of implementing these regulations, other good sources of information are local herpetological societies. It does not pay to break the law in this particular area. Before you know it, you could be making newspaper headlines and the 6 o'clock news. If local authorities call in the state or federal enforcement agencies (State Fish and Game and U.S. Fish and Wildlife) to investigate the possibility of other violations, you could also have an experience of personal violation that you are not about to forget. In some areas, possible possession of an illegal reptile can get more media attention than a major drug bust. Think about it. Some of you know what I'm talking about.

General Information

SCIENTIFIC NAME
The scientific name of the Burmese python is *Python molurus bivittatus*.

DISTRIBUTION
Indo-Chinese subregion (including Burma, Thailand, and Vietnam), Southern China, Hong Kong, Hainan, Borneo, Celebes, Java and Sumbawa. The great majority of Burmese pythons in the U.S. originally came from Thailand. A recently imported strain of albino Burmese captive-bred in Europe is said to have originated from Viet Nam.

PROTECTION
All pythons and boas including the Burmese python are considered threatened by the Convention on the International Trade in Endangered Species and listed under

Tame female Burmese python kept on display at Reptile Haven in Escondido, CA. Nearly 200lbs. and more than a single person can reasonably handle.

8

Albino and normal Burmese hatchlings. Photo by Bob Clark.

Appendix II. This means that special permits will be required for the import/export of these animals between countries. The related Indian python *Python molurus molurus* is considered endangered and listed as an Appendix I animal. It is also listed as endangered under the U.S. Endangered Species Act and therefor requires special permits for transport between countries as well as for ownership and movement of animals between states within the U.S.

For information on CITES and ESA permits and regulations, write to:
the U.S. Fish and Wildlife Service, Federal Permit Office, 1001 N. Glebe Rd, Room 611, Arlington VA 22201.

Burmese pythons are now protected in Thailand and consequently relatively few wild collected animals are being imported into the U.S.

SIZE
Hatchling Burmese pythons measure between 18 inches (runts) and 29 inches. Breeders indicate an average length of 22 inches among captive-bred animals. The average weight of hatchlings will be around 4oz (115g). Female Burmese pythons can grow to between 13 and 18 feet and there are records of animals over 19 feet but no authenticated records of animals over 20 feet. Males are typically smaller and their lengths range from 8 to 14 feet though occasionally a male will grow to a length of 16-17 feet (Bob Clark pers. comm). For their size, Burmese pythons are among the heaviest of the giant snakes with 17-18 foot animals achieving weights of over 200 lbs.

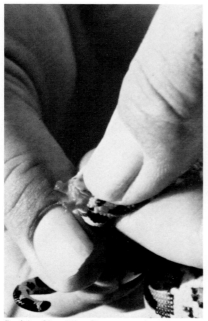

Sexing of hatchling Burmese pythons by manually attempting to evert hemipenes in potential males. The animal on the left is a male (note everted hemipenes). The animal on the right is a female.

SEXING

Hatchling Burmese pythons are easily sexed by manually everting the hemipenes in males. With this method, a hatchling python is held in such a way that the hind part of the body is positioned belly side up within the hand. The thumb should hold the area just in front of the vent (opening to the cloaca) against the index. The base of the tail (just past the vent) rests on the index finger. With the thumb of the other hand, using a gentle rolling motion and starting at an area about a half inch past the vent (base of the tail), roll the thumb while applying pressure toward the vent. If done correctly, this will cause the hemipenes to evert in males. The problem with this method is that it should only be performed by people experienced with the process. A snake can easily be injured by an inexperienced individual applying undue pressure to the area. As a backup, those individuals which appear to be females should be probed with a 1mm sexing probe. Females will probe to a depth of 3-5 subcaudal scales. Hatchling males will probe to a depth of 8-9 subcaudal scales. Adult males will probe to a depth of 10-16 subcaudals.

Adults can only be reliably sexed through probing though several characteristics such as larger size of females (usually), larger spurs to the sides of the vent in males and broader thicker tails in males can provide useful (but not always reliable) clues to the sex of animals. Besides probing, breeding behaviors are very good indicators of sex.

Probing adult Burmese pythons is a two person operation. One individual will have to control the snake being probed and firmly hold and present, belly side up, the vent area of the snake toward the individual performing the probing. One method which will help control large snakes and facilitate probing is to put the snake in a cloth snake bag allowing only the tail to remain outside. For Burmese pythons, 2-4 mm probes will work well depending on size. To probe a Burmese python the area just in front of the vent should be held with one hand and the thumb used to pull back the area in front (remember in front is towards the head) of the anal scale to expose the cloacal opening. With the other hand the probe, after moistening with clean water, should be gently inserted with a slight twirling motion into one of two small openings visible to the side of the cloacal opening. In adult females, the probe will enter a musk gland to a length of 3-5 subcaudal scales while, in adult males, it will enter an inverted hemipenis to a length of 10-16 subcaudal scales. To verify a reading, the process can be repeated on the other side. This is a procedure which is best performed and taught by experienced individuals. Most specialized reptile dealers will perform this service when you intend to buy animals of specific sexes.

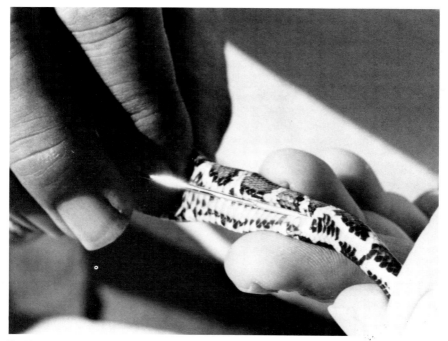

Probing a hatchling Burmese python.

GROWTH

Under captive conditions, Burmese pythons will grow to sexual maturity at an amazing rate. Growth rates achieved with females by herpetoculturists under optimal feeding conditions typically show the following growth pattern. By the end of 12 months, growth to a length of 6 to 9 1/2 feet. By 18 months, growth to between 9 and 10 1/2 feet. Breeding is initiated soon after this time and the growth rate from there on slows down considerably. Breeders mention growth rates of 12 to eighteen inches a year for the first 2-3 years following the ten foot mark (and thus first breeding). Thereafter, the growth rate will continue to decline with age though there are reports of older animals entering a period of accelerated growth following several years of typically reduced growth. There can be a wide range of variation in the growth and length of captive-raised specimens depending on genetic background, feeding and breeding regimens.

COLOR AND PATTERN MORPHS

Several color and pattern morphs of the Burmese python are currently being selectively bred by American herpetoculturists.

PATTERN MORPHS

Two pattern morphs are currently recognized by herpetoculturists. The normal and the "patternless" morph. The latter is in fact not truly patternless. Juveniles bear a pronounced broken middorsal stripe which fades as the animal matures leading to the term striped Burmese being employed by some herpetoculturists to describe this phase. The "patternless" Burmese also has a dilute brown coloration which has led to this morph also being called the "green" Burmese python. This dilute coloration can also appear independently of the "patternless" condition and is found in another morph of Burmese python which retains the normal pattern but with the dilute coloration. The few specimens in the herpetocultural trade with these characters are currently called "cinnamon" Burmese pythons.

A new pattern morph which will become more widespread in the not too distant future has been tentatively named the "Labyrinth" Burmese python. In this morph, the first 25 % of the body is striped while the rest has a complex and variable aberrant pattern.

COLOR MORPHS

Besides the standard wild coloration, the color morph which has gained the greatest popularity in recent years is the amelanistic albino Burmese python with normal pattern and bright white, yellow and orange coloration. Though the first specimens of this morph initially sold for several thousand dollars, the price of albino Burmese has been gradually declining and becoming more affordable to many herpetoculturists.

Recently, through selective breeding, a herpetoculturist in Michigan produced the first albino "patternless" Burmese python. There is currently one specimen in the U.S. (it is at the present time the only one known to exist) of a leucistic Burmese python which is an immaculate bright white with black eyes. It is hoped that in time this spectacular morph will eventually become established.

Because of the rapid maturation rate and high reproductive rate of Burmese pythons as well as a general interest by Burmese python breeders to segregate and selectively breed new morphs, we can expect many more varieties of Burmese pythons to appear in future years.

Leucistic Burmese python. Photo by Bob Clark.

Selecting a Burmese Python

The initial selection of a Burmese python is a critical first step which will determine the probability of your success at raising the animal to maturity as well as the long term relationship you will have with the animal. The following are guidelines which should help you select a potentially healthy Burmese python as well as one which will be likely to become a good pet with a docile personality.

CAPTIVE-BRED VERSUS WILD CAUGHT

The first choice when contemplating the purchase of a Burmese python should be a captive-bred hatchling from a reliable breeder. Captive-bred Burmese pythons are less likely to harbor diseases than imported Burmese pythons.

As a second choice, imported hatchling Burmese are the next best selection. As a precaution, it is recommended to have the stools of any imported Burmese checked for internal parasites including protozoans such as Entamoeba and Trichomonas. It is also a good idea to also have them checked for Salmonella.

SELECTING A BURMESE PYTHON

Whether you are buying a captive-bred or an imported Burmese python, careful attention should be given to the selection of an animal to determine visually and through handling the probability of its being healthy and the probability that it will be docile.

The following are guidelines for selection:

A. Prior to requesting that a specific animal be handed over to you for inspection, select animals that have rounded bodies and don't demonstrate pronounced backbone or rib definition. Check that the skin is relatively clear and free of superficial injuries.
Avoid runts.

B. Ask that the animal be handed over to you. Once in hand, a healthy Burmese python should give a distinct impression of strength and good muscle tone. Avoid animals that give an impression of limpness and poor muscle tone. The latter are always reliable indicators of poor health.

C. Next you should perform a series of steps to try to determine the health status of the animal:

Step 1.
Hold the snake behind the head with one hand and using the other hand, gently pull down the skin underneath the lower jaw to open the mouth of the animal. Look for the presence of bubbly mucus which will be a sign of a respiratory infection. Another technique to determine this but not as reliable, is to leave the mouth of the snake closed and using the thumb of the free hand, gently press up against the throat area. This will often cause mucus to emerge from the sides of the mouth or the nostrils in snakes with respiratory infections. Avoid snakes with these symptoms.

Step 2.
Repeating the procedure for opening the mouth, look for signs of mouthrot (stomatitis). This will appear as areas of gums covered with caseous (cheesy-looking) matter. In some cases red, raw and injured areas will be present. Again, avoid animals with these symptoms.

Step 3.
While in hand, check the eyes to make sure that they are clear. If the snake is in shed, both eyes should demonstrate equal levels of opacity (clouding over).

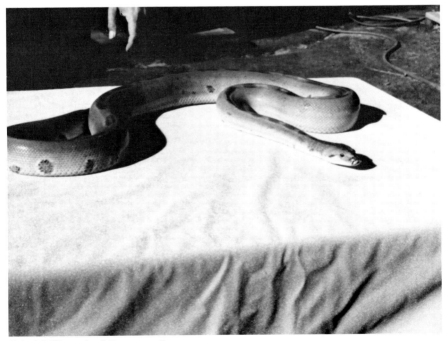

Subadult "Patternless" Burmese python.

Step 4.
Check for body lumps. Check the body for bumps and depressed areas along the backbone. Check for collapsed areas along the sides of the body. This is a sign of broken ribs. Avoid snakes with any of these symptoms.

Step 5.
Check the belly area to make sure that it is free of signs of skin infection (raised ventral scales, stained and damaged scales etc.)

Step 6.
Check the vent (opening to the cloaca) to make sure the anal scale lies flat against the body and is free of any caked or crusty matter. Make sure that the surrounding area is free of signs of smeared diarrhea. Avoid snakes with these symptoms.

Step 7.
Look for mites. These are tiny round, bead-like arthropods. When present, they can be seen moving on the body. They can also be seen imbedded between the rims of the eyes and the eyes themselves, giving a raised impression to the rims. Two reliable indicators of mites are the presence of scattered white flecks (mite feces) on the body of a snake and, following inspection of a snake, the presence of tiny mites crawling on one's hands. If you have other snakes in your collection, it is also recommended to avoid purchasing snakes with these parasites.

SELECTING FOR DOCILITY

Hatchling Burmese may initially be nippy. However, specimens which will become very docile tend to settle down, stop biting, and move more calmly after some gentle handling. At the other extreme are young Burmese that will try to get out of your hands as quickly as they can, will defecate, and when restrained, will bite repeatedly. Other animals will demonstrate behaviors which will range somewhere in between. If docility when handling is an important consideration in your selection then you should pay extra attention to this area when selecting animals.

TEMPERAMENT

No studies have been done to clearly determine the relationship of genetics to temperament in Burmese pythons. Many people have the notion that with handling, virtually any Burmese can become tame, but that is simply not true. In the opinion and experience of the author and other herpetoculturists, genetics plays a crucial role in the determination of "personality" in Burmese pythons. These differences in temperament are often obvious even when the animals are young. Some Burmese are simply nasty and even with regular handling remain nervous and likely to bite. Some have a calm disposition which is apparent early on and persists as the animal matures. Others are somewhere in between, not really nasty but not calm either and remain nervous when handled though they may be reluctant to bite. The author suspects that these traits of temperament are genetically determined and that selective breeding for good temperament by herpetoculturists is desirable if Burmese pythons are to become more widespread as reptile pets. With Burmese pythons, initial temperament plays a key role on subsequent human behavior rather than the other way around (human behavior influencing temperament). As a rule, the more docile a Burmese python is to start with, the more frequently it will be handled. On the other hand, the reverse is true, nasty Burmese get handled less frequently because their owners eventually dread the chore of having to deal with them. With Burmese pythons, personality should be at least as important as looks. How about 14 feet of nasty good looks to deal with on a weekly basis?

Burmese python constricting a rabbit; a very different beast than the hatchling which could once have fit in a pocket. Photo by Robert Applegate.

17

Housing and Maintenance

LOCATION OF ENCLOSURES

Because Burmese pythons become such large animals, it is important that their enclosures be placed in a room with plenty of wide open space to facilitate maintenance and handling of these animals. An adult Burmese python in a cluttered room can readily topple furniture in the course of handling. From a safety point of view, a cluttered room will not allow you the maneuverability recommended to safely and responsibly maintain and handle these animals. It is recommended that any room where snakes are maintained be kept locked when the owners are not present. This will prevent possible tampering by children or guests. If the room is inspected and modified to take care of holes in the wall and other openings and if care is taken to methodically shut windows when leaving the room, a locked room will contain a snake in case of an escape (unlikely if you were a responsible herpetoculturist and had an appropriate enclosure with a locking mechanism).

Custom-made 8 foot long enclosures for housing adult Burmese pythons. These are front opening with a locking mechanism clearly visible at the upper part of each door.

ENCLOSURES

Enclosures for Burmese pythons should be specifically designed for housing snakes. These should have either a sliding or hinged cover or sliding or hinged front (either clear plexiglas panels or framed plexiglas or 1/4 inch tempered glass doors) with a locking mechanism which prevents any risk of accidental escape by the snake. Such locking mechanisms will vary depending on the enclosure design i.e a latch that prevents accidental opening of a sliding plexiglas front. Virtually all escapee large constrictors are the result of

18

inadequate housing at home or during transport ("It got out of the bag. The damn thing had a hole in the side, I hadn't noticed, oops"). Common stupid practices for covering the cages of large snakes are to place boards on top with rocks or books to keep the cover down. This method doesn't work and is irresponsible. If you can't build or buy an adequate cage, then you shouldn't own the snake.

A big problem in the pet trade is that many stores except for those who specialize in reptiles do not carry enclosures suitable for housing snakes. Many still sell the standard glass tank with screen cover and no good method for keeping the cover down. So purchase, build or have built an enclosure specifically designed for securely housing snakes or other reptiles and make sure it has a locking mechanism.

A section of the python breeding facilities at the Dehesa Valley Animal Center in El Cajon, CA. On the left are multiple 8 foot enclosures. On the right are wood frames with vinyl-coated welded wire walk-in enclosures.

At the time of writing, virtually no commercial snake enclosure is readily available in the trade suitable for housing large adult Burmese pythons except some of the large enclosures offered by Neodesha Plastics®. This means that you will probably have to build or hire a woodworker to build a suitable enclosure.

ENCLOSURE SIZE

For hatchling Burmese, an enclosure the size of a standard ten gallon aquarium could be adequate, except that Burmese grow so fast that within one year, an enclosure at least 36 inches long and 18 inches wide will be required. By two years, an enclosure at least 48 inches long and 24 inches wide will be required and preferably an enclosure 60- 84 inches long (the size enclosure a female will eventually require). These are not enclosure sizes readily available in stores and you will ultimately find that you have few choices other than having a enclosure built (one exception is the large cage manufactured by Neodesha Plastics®

19

mentioned above). Other than the standard wood and glass/plexiglas cages, some breeders have successfully used vinyl coated welded wire attached to wood framing to construct large efficient walk-in enclosures for housing and breeding large numbers of pythons.

GROUND MEDIUM

To make a fancy attractive set-up for a Burmese would require no less than a room-sized enclosure. Because of this, virtually all herpetoculturists choose to keep Burmese pythons under simple, easily maintained conditions. Using plants for decoration is virtually out of the question unless you have enough room to plant some large trees or shrubs (very unlikely). As a ground medium, select one that is easily replaced such as pine shavings newspaper, rabbit pellets (alfalfa) or fine orchid bark. The latter looks the most natural but should be thoroughly rinsed to remove any bark dust if one wishes to have a clean looking Burmese. If you have any notions of using anything fancy, just remember that when a big Burmese defecates we are talking copious amounts of semi-solid and liquid matter. Not necessarily a big deal in a room-sized enclosure but in a relatively small enclosure, the relative importance visually and olfactorily increase considerably. Simple, quick and easy to clean are the best solutions.

Dry landscape materials can be used for decoration as long as they can be easily cleaned or removed. These can include select pieces of wood, large sections of cork bark or dried grasses. For many reasons, including ease of handling, any decoration should be simple uncluttered and easily removed.

TEMPERATURE

Burmese pythons should be maintained at a temperature of 85-90F. But the issue of providing adequate heat is not so simple. The best system is to provide a daytime air temperature of 84-88F with a basking/heating area achieving a surface temperature of 88-92F. By providing a heated area, you will allow a Burmese python the opportunity to self-regulate its body temperature. At night, the air temperature can be allowed to drop to 80-84F. In emergency situations, the nighttime temperature can safely be allowed to drop to 65F for brief periods of time (several hours). As long as a heating/basking area is available many of the problems associated with temperatures that are too cool (respiratory infections, inability to effectively digest food, increased susceptibility to disease) can be avoided.

During pre-breeding conditioning, Burmese pythons will have to be maintained at cooler temperatures for several weeks (see chapter on Breeding).

Enclosure units, including a rolling holding box for easy cage cleaning used by Ernie Wagner.
Photo courtesy of Ernie Wagner.

THERMOMETERS

Many herpetoculturists tend to play a guessing game where temperature is concerned. They guesstimate the temperature of their room, of their set-ups and of the basking areas.

Thermometers are useful tools which should be used by all herpetoculturists. Currently several types of thermometers are available. They range from the standard enclosed mercury thermometers to stick on thermographic thermometers (some companies are now selling wide-range thermometers of this type for use with reptiles) to electronic thermometers. The author's favorite and most recommended thermometer for keeping reptiles are the electronic thermometers with sensors and an alarm which will warn you when the measured temperature is outside of the range that you set. These electronic thermometers are sold in electronic supply stores for twenty to thirty-five dollars (depending on their features) at the time of writing. At one setting, you can get a continuous visual read out of the room temperature. By switching the setting, you can also get a visual read-out of the temperature through the sensor (which can be placed on such things as a basking/heating area or inside an incubator) provided. At the push of a button

21

some of these thermometers will also give you the minimum/maximum reading over twenty-four hours. These electronic thermometers are invaluable toherpetoculturists and should be used more widely.

HEATING SYSTEMS USED BY HERPETOCULTURISTS

1. Space heaters/room heaters.
These types of heaters, easily obtainable from most department and hardware stores, are frequently used by many herpetoculturists maintaining large collections. All things considered, they are still one of the best and most economical systems for heating a room but they do have problems. Virtually all of the problems have to do with the risk of overheating. Every year there is at least one story of an individual losing his/her entire collection because "The damn thermostat on the thing failed and it kept running. I lost every snake in the place." A recent incident involved a python breeder who lost virtually every Burmese python in his possession including albino Burmese. The lesson here is that a system has do be devised to prevent this type of thing to happen. Either purchase a thermostat or set up an alarm that will warn you when the temperature goes over a set temperature. Aside from thermostats failing, one cause of heaters failing to perform satisfactorily involves their placement. If you place a heater on the floor where there is a cool draft, the thermostat on the heater senses the cool floor temperature instead of the room temperature causing the heater to keep on running. Also remember that a room heater will create heat gradients with temperatures near the ceiling as much as 10F higher than temperatures near the ground. One practice that can help reduce the incidence of thermostat failure is to replace heaters on a regular basis. Some individuals will do it every year as standard practice.. Thermostats are more likely to fail on old heaters.

So take notice of the above warning and buy thermometers and thermostats and do what you have to do. Don't procrastinate, this is serious stuff. Heed this warning (how many times do I have to say it ?).

Note: Read instructions carefully regarding heater use and be careful and responsible in terms of its placement. Think fire prevention.

2. Hot Rocks
As a rule "hot rock" type heaters can present problems for snakes.
However, at least some brands of " hot rocks" if used properly can be used when raising hatchling pythons. They key is to measure surface temperature which should be 85-95F. If the surface temperature exceeds 95F, piace a thin flat rock on top to diffuse the surface heat, measure the temperature again. If it is within

the appropriate range, this system will be suitable for raising hatchling and juvenile Burmese. Eventually the snake will outgrow any size "hot rock" you might purchase and you will have to resort to other heating systems.

3. Incandescent lights
Incandescent bulbs, spotlights, or floodlights in an appropriate fixture can also be used to keep pythons warm. The important point is to measure the temperature at the basking area immediately underneath the fixture/bulb and at the distance furthest from the bulb after the bulb will have been on a for at least an hour.

Extreme care must be given to assure that the fixture and bulb are placed outside of the cage with screening preventing any possible direct contact with the bulb. Snakes are not normally exposed to searing heat in the wild and they tend to be stupid in terms of judging their tolerance to hot surfaces. Thermal burns, involving poorly placed and protected fixture/light systems, are a common veterinary problem with captive reptiles. So think snake and keep that bulb away.

Note: Be sure to place the fixture/bulb in such a way that no object, cloth, etc., is likely to make contact with the bulb or unit. Think fire prevention.

4. Heating pads
Standard heating pads set at a low to medium setting (use thermometer) can be used with pythons up to a certain size. Currently some companies are also selling heating pads specifically for use with reptiles. When used at the right setting and in the right manner, these are a good heating systems for smaller pythons. Read instructions carefully as to proper use.

5. Pig blankets/fiberglass heating pads
You may have never heard of these but these are the best commercially produced heating units for large reptiles. These are sold or can be special ordered through feed stores. They are large (usually at least 3 feet x 1 foot) rigid fiberglass enclosed units that provide a high surface heat over a broad area. For use with large reptiles, these units must be controlled with an appropriate thermostat which can be special ordered from the manufacturer.

Some herpetoculturists, after carefully determining the position of the heating elements within the fiberglass, will bolt one of these units on a piece of plywood raised above 12" legs to create a heated platform. When keeping more than one python in a large cage, this heated platform will provide a heated area for a python lying on top as well as overhead heating for the animal using the underside as a shelter. Before making any such modifications for your personal use, read instructions carefully and if necessary contact the manufacturing company for any additional information as to proper use. For keeping large pythons warm, there is nothing like them.

MAINTENANCE

A weekly maintenance schedule should be implemented with Burmese pythons . Clean the enclosure to remove feces and replace areas of soiled ground medium as needed. The water container should be cleaned and disinfected and the water replaced at least on a weekly basis.

TOOLS

Many herpetoculturists resort to several tools for maintaining their Burmese pythons. One of the most widely used tools for handling large snakes are snake hooks which can be purchased from specialized dealers. Other tools used to maintain Burmese pythons will include various "shields" which are custom made by herpetoculturists to suit their purposes. A shield will usually consist of a section of plexiglas or plywood with a handle attached to it's center. Some herpetoculturists will also put a 4 inch lip around the shield. Some use both small and large shields. Plexiglas® shields or wood shields with a section of Plexiglas® in their center have the advantage of providing visibility. Typical uses of shields are to create a barrier between oneself and a snake when removing food or cleaning litter. Large shields with a 4 inch wide lip can be placed on a coiled Burmese while cleaning the cage or when removing eggs. The need to use tools will vary depending on one's set-ups, the nature and number of animals one is working with and the maintenance routines one has established.

Feeding

Following hatching, Burmese pythons will begin to feed soon after their first shed. As a rule, Burmese pythons feed readily at all sizes and present no problems in this area. The best and most readily available food for Burmese pythons are commercially-bred rodents starting with mice when they are hatchlings, then rats of an appropriate size and eventually rabbits. Most Burmese pythons will readily feed on both live and prekilled animals. As a rule, it is recommended to feed prekilled rodents to prevent any possible injury to the snake and to minimize suffering in the prey animal.

SIZE OF PREY - GUIDELINES

As a rule apparent width of a prey item should not be greater than the greatest apparent width measured at midbody of the snake to be fed. It is important to feed prey items of the appropriate size. Prey items that are too large may be eaten but run a high risk of being regurgitated at a later time.

Thus, hatchlings should initially be fed just weaned mice. After a few feedings, you can offer adult mice. If you offer prey of adequate size, you can start by feeding your snake one prey item and then introducing a second prey item. If your Burmese python is still hungry, it may feed on a second prey item. If not, it will usually leave it alone. By the time they are four feet, Burmese pythons should be fed small rats and should gradually be offered bigger rats as they become larger. By the time they reach six to seven feet, they can be switched from large rats to small rabbits. As they grow older Burmese should gradually be fed larger rabbits.

LIVE OR PREKILLED

Burmese can be fed prekilled prey from the time they are hatchlings. The advantage to feeding prekilled prey is that it minimizes suffering in the prey animal and it minimizes the possibility of bites and damage to a pet python. It also makes offering and removing a prey animal easier. One method of humanely killing mice and rats is to grab one by the tail and with a swift motion strike the back of the head against the edge of a table. With rabbits, the best method is to ask your supplier to kill them at the time of purchase. It is recommended that all prey animals be offered live or prekilled soon after removal from their rearing cages. It has been suggested that vitamin C and other nutrients from food remaining in the prey animal's guts may be beneficial to snakes. As with all predators, when a snake ingests it's prey, it also ingests the gut contents of the prey. Thus, care should be given to assure that prey animals are fed a high quality diet. Vitamin C which can be provided by gut contents has been shown to play a role in reducing the probability of stomatitis (mouthrot) and in maintaining the integrity of the skin.

OTHER FOODS

Some herpetoculturists occasionally feed their Burmese prekilled whole chickens. The fact is that Burmese pythons, like many other larger snakes, like fowl of any type. In SE Asia, Burmese pythons kept as pets or on display are often maintained on a diet consisting primarily of fowl (captive-bred rats and rabbits are not readily available in Asian countries). Burmese pythons which for one reason or another are off-feed will often feed with great enthusiasm on chickens. And most Burmese will readily feed on raw chicken parts such as chicken thighs or drumsticks right from the market. But caution should be used when feeding fowl in any form. A significant percentage of raw chicken parts sold in markets will test positive for salmonella. If feeding live or prekilled chickens, care must be given to the selection of the source. The best would be to raise chickens at home under relatively hygienic conditions. Many herpetoculturists prekill any fowl and freeze them for several weeks prior to feeding. The effectiveness of this procedure has not been clearly determined.

As a rule, fowl should be only be used as a resort for fattening Burmese pythons which are reluctant to feed. (i.e., an import or to put on that extra bit of weight right before pre-breeding conditioning).

FEEDING REGIMENS

The growth of your Burmese python will be directly related to its feeding regimen (all other conditions being adequate i.e., temperature). The growth rate of Burmese pythons is greatest during the first eighteen months to three years (at which point they will reach sexual maturity) and thereafter slows down considerably though Burmese pythons can and will grow for most of their lives.

The feeding regimen of a Burmese python should be adjusted to its growth rate and overall appearance/condition. A standard procedure involves optimal feeding (some herpetoculturists use the term power-feed) for the first two to three years and then cutting down on the regimen when growth rate slows down to prevent the risk of obesity. Adjustments are also made with breeding females to optimize breeding condition. As a rule, females should have good weight but should not be obese for good breeding results. Following egg-laying, females are often fed more frequently to make up for weight loss. These are all factors which must be taken into account when determining feeding regimens.

STANDARD FEEDING REGIMENS

From hatchling to four feet: Feed one to two mice of an appropriate size every three to four days.

From four feet to sexual maturity (point where relative growth rate begins to slow; usually around 10 feet in females and around 8 feet in males): Feed one to two prey animals every five-seven days.

At four feet: Switch to medium rats, then slowly graduate to larger rats. By six to seven feet, switch to three pound rabbits. Increase the size of the rabbit(s) as the animal grows.

From sexual maturity (app. 18 months) to three years: Feed one to two rabbits once a week.

From three years on: Feed one to two rabbits every ten days, with adjustments depending on overall appearance of animal. Animals that are bred every year and allowed to brood eggs may have to be fed every week to regain enough weight in six months to be able to breed the following year. Use your judgment.

26

STUNTING

Burmese pythons that are fed infrequently or offered small amounts of food per feeding during the first 12 to 18 months of life will be seriously stunted and may require several years to achieve a size suitable for breeding. These animals often remain stunted for life never achieving a normal size for the species. Some of these animals during the course of such a starvation program will also tend to be aggressive (who can blame them?).

THE RIGHT WAY TO FEED BURMESE PYTHONS

Up to a length of six feet, Burmese pythons can be fed without special precautions other than being careful when placing or removing food from the cage. But once they reach a size greater than six feet it is critical that a herpetoculturist adopt safe feeding procedures to prevent the possibility of injury to himself.

The following are sound feeding procedures:

1. Only house one snake per cage and thus feed only one snake per cage at a time.

2. Have prey items within reach. Determine where the snake is before opening door. The snake should be away from the door. If it is near the door, have a snake stick ready to move the snake away from the door. Open door, move snake away from the vicinity of the door with snake stick. Then grab the prey and toss the prey item from a distance onto a suitable site in the cage or introduce the prey item with a long pair of snake tongs. Under no circumstance should you hold a prey item by the tail or scruff of the neck to offer the snake until it strikes it out of your hand. Don't be stupid.

3. If the snake doesn't feed and you have to remove the prey, open the cage and, using a large snake stick, push the snake away from the vicinity of the prey and push the prey item toward the door. Remove the prey with a large set of tongs. Remove the prey with your hand only if the snake is at the other end of a large cage and well out of possible striking range of your hand or the prey item you are grabbing. A safe method is to place a small wood board or a shield between the snake and yourself prior to removing any prey item.

WATER

Burmese pythons in the wild are often found near water. In captivity, water should regularly be made available in a large sturdy water bowl or, if one can afford the space, in a small pool.
Aside from the necessity of providing water, a water container will also raise the air humidity in the vivarium and will provide an area for soaking that will facilitate proper shedding of the skin.

A problem when using large pools involves cleaning since Burmese pythons will frequently defecate in a container of water. All efforts should be made to be able to provide water in a container that can be regularly cleaned and disinfected in a 5% chlorine solution (unscented bleach from the supermarket). Containers that are allowed to remain foul will encourage the growth of microorganisms that can lead to disease. It is best to establish maintenance procedures and routines that allow for regularly providing clean water in clean containers.

Breeding

Burmese pythons are among the easiest to breed of all snakes. They can reach sexual maturity by 18 months of age and have a relatively high reproductive rate.

PRE-BREEDING FACTORS

Prior to breeding Burmese pythons, one should make sure that one has properly sexed pairs, that they are of a size which makes it highly probable that they are sexually mature and that any animals selected for breeding are disease free and have adequate weight. It is generally recommended that female Burmese pythons be slightly overweight prior to breeding. Underweight, obviously thin females should not be bred.

Minimum recommended breeding size for female Burmese pythons is nine and a half feet, larger is preferable. Males should be at least 8 feet though some males are sexually mature at 7 feet.

BREEDING AGE

Burmese pythons if captive-raised and optimally fed will be sexually mature by 18 months of age. But some breeders who are not as eager to breed their animals as quickly as possible prefer waiting an extra year or two before breeding their female Burmese pythons. The result is being able to keep female Burmese on a nearly year round feeding schedule for that extra one or two years. Within that period of time these females can achieve an extra foot or more in length compared to early-bred Burmese, which once they begin breeding, will be off feed four to six months out of a year. Some breeders claim that the benefits of delaying breeding are larger females which, once they begin breeding, will consistently produce larger clutches compared to early-bred Burmese pythons.

On the other hand, some of the top Burmese python breeders in the U.S. claim that in the long run there is no significant difference in reproductive performance between early-bred and later-bred Burmese pythons. To a great degree, the maintenance schedule and the consequent size and weight of one's animals (particularly females), should be the determining factors as to whether they are ready to breed.

BREEDING PROFILES

Optimal breeding frequency in Burmese pythons will tend to occur within the first few years following sexual maturity. As animals get larger and older, some may not necessarily breed every year but will occasionally skip a year and eventually may skip more than a year between breedings. The fact is that there is variation in Burmese pythons in terms of their breeding potential. Some females will breed every year for ten years in a row while others will routinely skip years. Some females as they become older may stop breeding altogether. Though older animals may breed less frequently than younger animals, they often will make up for it by producing large numbers of eggs. Not enough data is available to present a long term profile of intensive captive breeding of Burmese pythons. In time, enough information will be available to determine optimal breeding schedules, breeding age and the point where Burmese may become past their prime and past optimal economic returns.

PRE-BREEDING CONDITIONING

Prior to breeding, Burmese pythons should be exposed to a cool rest period for 4 to 8 weeks. During that time, the basking/heating unit is turned off and the enclosure temperature determined exclusively by air temperature. Many herpetoculturists cool their Burmese pythons on a schedule beginning any time between Oct. 15 and Jan. 1 by allowing the temperature in their cages to drop down to a minimum of 65F (low 70's is the most desirable) at night with maximum daytime temperatures in the lower 80's. Some breeders also use a method whereby the room temperature (and thus air temperature in the enclosure) is maintained at a temperature of 75-78F round the clock during the cooling period. During that time the animals are carefully monitored to assure that they do not develop respiratory infections.

This pre-breeding conditioning is essential for consistent and controlled breeding of Burmese pythons. During this period, the Burmese pythons are not fed. The cooling is believed to alter the metabolic pathways in females such that they ovulate following cooling and stored fat is converted to maturing eggs. In males cooling is believed to lead to an increase in male hormone, the resulting breeding behavior and fertility through the production of healthy and active spermatozoa.

BREEDING

Following the pre-breeding conditioning, the temperature is raised back to normal and female animals are placed back on a high frequency feeding schedule (food offered every five days). Male Burmese pythons will typically fast following cooling and through the actual breeding period. Starting about three weeks after return to a normal schedule, the female is introduced into a male's cage. Some herpetoculturists at this point keep pairs together while others remove and reintroduce pairs allowing them to spend a couple of days together once to twice a week. By introducing or pairing a female alternately with more than one male, chances of high fertility will be increased. Copulation once initiated will last for several hours. Once mating activity begins, females will usually stop feeding.

An alternative method to induce breeding used by some breeders is to keep animals at a temperature of 75-78F during the prebreeding conditioning and during breeding for a total period of 8-10 weeks. With this method, females are not put back on a standard feeding schedule and the animals are introduced or kept in pairs beginning with the fourth week following the initiation of cooling. By the end of the 8-10 week cooling period, females will usually be gravid.

Gravid females will continue to fast during the entire period of egg development and, if allowed to incubate their eggs, will continue to fast up to the time of hatching, a total fasting period which can last up to six months. If one incubates the eggs artificially, females can be induced to resume feeding by moving them regularly away from a spot where they may initiate brooding/incubation behavior (many females will persist to brood for varying periods of time even though their eggs will have been removed).

Egg-laying will usually occur two to three months following the observation of copulations. Many breeders will provide a shallow nest box with barely moist spaghnum moss as an egg-laying site (see maternal incubation). The female will undergo a pre-egglaying shed two to four weeks (most herpetoculturists report four weeks-30days) prior to egg-laying. Depending on their prebreeding conditioning and breeding schedules, breeders have reported females laying eggs between January and July but most eggs of Burmese pythons in captivity are laid between February and June.

NUMBER OF EGGS LAID

Depending on size, weight and other factors, the number of eggs laid by a female Burmese python will vary. As a rule, the larger the female, the more eggs she will lay. At a size of nine and a half to ten and a half feet when first breeding may be initiated, females will typically lay from eighteen to twenty-five eggs but there are reports of 42-45 eggs being laid by females bred at an age of eighteen months. During the second year of breeding, egg clutches will typically range from 25-38 eggs with many reports of significantly larger clutches. As females grow larger, more eggs are usually produced (also dependent on the overall condition including fat reserves) . There is a record of a large female Burmese python laying a clutch of 107 eggs.

Female Burmese python incubating a clutch of eggs. Photo by Robert Applegate.

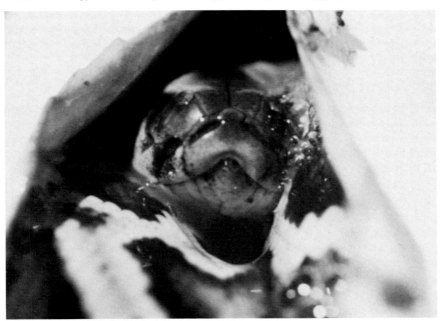

Burmese python hatchling having just slit the shell of the egg. Note the egg-tooth just underneath the snout. Photo by Robert Applegate.

INCUBATION

There are two widely used methods for incubating the eggs of Burmese and other pythons.

1. Maternal incubation

A method increasingly used by herpetoculturists is to allow the females to incubate their eggs. To do this, a nestbox consisting of a wood frame 2 feet x 2 feet and 6 inches tall is placed inside the female's enclosure. Within 2 weeks following the pre-egglaying shed the frame or open box is then filled with 3-4 inches of moistened sphagnum moss. When the time is right, most females will invariably lay their clutch and coil within the nestbox to brood their eggs. The room or the enclosure should be maintained at a temperature of 84-87F. It is important not to keep the female too warm and to provide a temperature range which will allow her to regulate incubation temperature. Female Burmese pythons can through "shivering" and other behaviors raise the temperature within their coils several degrees above the ambient air temperature. However, a female can do little to cool down eggs when the temperature is too high.

A problem, when allowing maternal incubation, involves the possible dehydration of the eggs. Typically, breeders will mist (with a hand sprayer) the snake and eggs daily with a thorough spraying of the moss. Some breeders will strategically place some clear plastic over the eggs and/or snake to reduce evaporative rate. Increasing the relative humidity of the room with a humidifier will be beneficial. Allowing maternal brooding is not recommended with females which appear too thin following egg laying because a female will not feed during the entire incubation period which will last approximately two months.

2. Artificial incubation

Another method used by many breeders is to remove the eggs following laying and place them in an incubator maintained at 88-90F. A widely used type of incubator involves using a submersible aquarium heater in an aaquarium with shallow water just a few inches above the submersible heater which will have been placed on the floor of the aquarium. With the help of an aquarium thermometer the heater is calibrated to heat the water at the desired temperature (additional adjustments will have to be made later. Above the water area, a platform is constructed, using plexiglas or bricks or welded wire, on which the container of eggs will be placed.

The container in which the python eggs are placed is filled with 2-3 inches of moistened vermiculite (equal parts of water and vermiculite by weight) and the eggs are placed on their side on top of the vermiculite. Inside the container, a small vessel of water (i.e., a small jar with water) should be placed to help maintain a high relative air humidity. The container is then covered with the lid which should be perforated with a few holes to allow for air exchange. A thermometer should be placed in the container. One type of thermometer that is very effective for incubators are the electronic digital readout thermometers with outdoor sensors sold in electronic supply stores. Simply place the sensor/probe inside the container and switch the thermometer to the out reading. This will give you a continuous reading of the temperature inside the container. A back up aquarium thermometer in the water and against the glass should be used. Electronic thermometers do occasionally fail. Place the container on the platform inside the "incubator" and cover the aquarium with a glass or plexiglas cover allowing a very small (1/4') open space for air exchange. Some herpetoculturists will make a styrofoam cover to provide better insulation. Over the next few hours carefully monitor the temperature inside the container and calibrate, using small adjustments, the submersible heater until the desired temperature is achieved. Do not neglect calibration of the incubator. If the temperature becomes too high, you could end up cooking your eggs. Proper calibration will take time so resign yourself to it. On the other hand, once the incubator is calibrated, it can be used in the future with little or no further adjustments. The temperature should be monitored at least twice daily. The eggs should be monitored and examined briefly at least twice a week. They will hatch in approximately two months (57-63 days).

Burmese pythons hatching. Photo by Ernie Wagner.

Diseases and Disorders

MITES

These tiny external parasites are the plague of snake keepers. Once present in a collection, complete eradication is often difficult. Unfortunately Burmese pythons once exposed, readily harbor these parasites. The presence of mites can be determined as follows:

1. Under a good light, check the surface of the skin of the Burmese python for tiny dark bead-like or flattened "bugs" crawling about the body. You can also notice the presence of mites by examining your hands following handling.

2. Check for the presence of fine white flecks (mite feces) on the body. Usually, with closer inspection, you will eventually find live mites.

3. Check the rim of the eyes. Burmese pythons with mites have rims that stick out from the eyes, the result of mites embedded in that area. If left untreated, Burmese pythons infected with mites will eventually die. Mites reproduce at a fast logarithmic rate and a Burmese python can in time harbor thousands of these blood-sucking parasites which will eventually kill snakes by causing anemia and dehydration. Thus, prompt treatment is essential.

A methodical manner for treating mites is as follows:
1. Take the snake out of its enclosure and place it in a container with shallow water (approximately the height of the body at its thickest point) for three to four hours. The container should be closed so as to prevent escape.

2. Take out all the cage furniture and ground medium from the cage. Disinfect any landscape features by soaking in a 3% bleach solution. Throw away the ground medium.

3. Take the snake out of the soaking container, wipe it with a cloth and place it back in the cage. Introduce, a section of Vapona® pest strip impregnated with 2.2 dichlorovinyl dimethy phosphate, (1" x 2" if in a small cage and 2" x 2" if in a large cage, larger sections in room-sized enclosures) in a plastic container perforated with holes. Seal cage ventilation holes except for a narrow strip to allow for some air exchange. Leave for 24 hours. Check that mites are on floor of cage and that no live mites remain before removing strip. If any live mites are still present, leave another 24 hours.

4. With a cloth on which a pyrethrin spray has been applied, thoroughly wipe the outside of the cage. Reinfection usually occurs as a result of mites which have crawled outside through ventilation areas. In time, these mites can return and reinfect the snake.

Repeat treatment in 10 days.

INTERNAL PARASITES

If one purchases imported Burmese pythons, a routine stool check for internal parasites should be performed by a qualified veterinarian. Imported Burmese pythons can harbor nematodes, trematodes and cestode worms. They can also be infected with protozoan parasites as well as with diseases organisms such as Salmonella.

Captive-bred and raised pythons are usually parasite free when maintained in a sanitary manner and fed on a diet of commercially raised rodents. Occasionally captive-bred and raised animals may become infected with high numbers of flagellate protozoans such as Trichomonas.

STOMATITIS/ MOUTHROT

This is a mouth infection usually caused by Pseudomonas. Typical symptoms include in the earlier stages, excessive mucus and enlarged or ruptured capillaries in the gum area. Eventually an area of caseous (cheesy-looking) matter builds up. In the earlier stages, this is easily treated by washing out the infected area daily with Betadyne® solution or Hydrogen peroxide or Listerine®. If left untreated, the disease will eventually spread and destroy gum and bone and result in loss of teeth. In advanced stages, topical treatment must be supported by injections of antibiotics such as Amikacin®. The latter will require the assistance of a veterinarian. The best is to catch it early.

Vitamin C administered by supplementing the food of the rodent prey can help reduce the probability of this disease. It is a good idea to feed rodents soon after removal from their rearing cages so that they still have food which may contain vitamin C in their gut.

SKIN BLISTER DISEASE

This is a skin disease that occurs when animals are kept under conditions that are damp and or dirty. Typical symptoms include raised scales with white bumps. Skin blister disease can be caused by several bacteria. In early stages when just a few infected areas are present, simply changing the housing conditions will lead to improvement. For this, the ground medium should be removed and the affected animal(s) should be kept on dry newspaper. The water dish should be removed and only placed in the enclosure twice a week for a few hours to provide water. In time the snake will shed out the damaged areas and will return to normal. In more serious cases, aside from changing housing conditions, one should apply Betadine® solution daily to the affected areas. In very serious cases, administering injectable antibiotics will become necessary.

SHEDDING PROBLEMS

Burmese pythons that are maintained in the proper manner do not usually have problems shedding as long as a large water container is available for soaking during the preshed (when eyes and skin become opaque) period. Any shedding problems can usually be remedied by allowing for soaking and removing unshed skin pieces by hand. Some snakes that have problems shedding may have other problems such as mites, skin blister disease or other disease. Sick snakes may also have problems shedding because they are too ill or weak to adequately perform the behaviors required for normal shedding. When problems with shedding occur, one must seek to remedy any associated environmental or health conditions.

Pythons that have problems shedding may retain shed skin on the head including the eye caps. Before removing eyecaps (spectacle shields), the snake must be allowed to soak for several hours to soften the eyecaps. Then, very carefully, with the use of rounded tweezers or forceps one can remove the eyecap by finding the edge of the eyecap along the eye rim, grasping it between the forceps, and very gently removing it from the eye. If the eye cap is not softened and the procedure not done properly one can cause serious and permanent injury to the eye. If in doubt, consult a more experienced herpetoculturist or a qualified veterinarian.

RESPIRATORY DISORDERS

Respiratory disorders are commonly found among imported Burmese pythons and, depending on several factors, can occur at various times with captive animals. Usually, exposure to cool temperatures is an associated factor. Early symptoms typically include the presence of bubbly mucus in the mouth, listlessness and loss of appetite. With time, the amount of mucus increases and the snake begins to gape with forced exhalations. As the diseases progresses, snakes will gape and keep their head partially raised. If untreated, respiratory infections can be fatal. The best is to notice the symptoms early on. When noticed early, (slight amount of bubbly mucus in mouth) the simplest initial treatment is to raise the cage temperature to a constant 88-90F. If the condition worsens or persists for more than a week, then a veterinarian should be consulted for the administration of an injectable antibiotic such as Amikacin®.

ENTERITIS

Typical symptoms of enteritis may include repeated regurgitation of ingested prey, loose,smelly and atypically colored stools, the presence of blood in the stools, loss of appetite, dehydration weight loss and listlessness. When enteritis is suspected, the only effective solution is to have a stool check and cultures performed by a veterinarian who will then be able to prescribe an effective medication. Common causes of enteritis in Burmese pythons include amoebiosis, flagellate protozoans and salmonella.

STAR GAZING DISEASE

This is a disease which can develop in imported animals but seldom occurs in captive-raised animals unexposed to imported snakes. Typical symptoms include periods of raising of the head perpendicular to the body. The cause is amebic involvement of the nervous system leading to meningoencephalitis. Causal organisms are amebaean protozoans, principally Acanthamoeba. Some success has been had by treating the animals with high dosages of Flagyl® (metronidazole) at up to 200mg/kg.

Hatchling "Labyrinth" Burmese pythons. Photo by Bob Clark.

How Accidents Happen

If maintained in a responsible manner and properly handled, Burmese pythons are relatively safe and predictable animals. But the same can be said of dogs. Yet every year millions of dollars are spent in the treatment of dog bites and 10-15 people a year are killed by dogs.

The most common misconception with captive-raised Burmese is that they are tame and therefore will not bite and will not constrict humans because they can recognize humans as harmless and... therefore will not demonstrate aggressive behavior towards them. This may be true under most circumstances but nothing changes the fact that Burmese pythons are not very smart creatures and that they remain after all large snakes with the interpretational systems characteristic of snakes and not humans.

EXAMPLES OF HOW ACCIDENTS CAN HAPPEN

* **Poor feeding practices** i.e., offering or removing prey animals by hand leading to accidental biting and constricting. Another common cause of accidents involves opening a cage to pick up a Burmese python after one has been handling rats or rabbits for the last fifteen minutes while feeding other snakes. Pythons recognize prey animals primarily by scent. If that hand doesn't look like a rabbit but sure smells like one than by God it must be fair prey. Oops.

* **Allowing a Burmese python to form a complete loop around one's neck.** Under certain circumstances simply by tightening its muscles to retain its balance, a large constrictor can apply enough pressure to lead to temporary suffocation and stop blood flow to the brain possibly resulting into loss of consciousness.

As a general rule with handling any large constrictors:
DO NOT ALLOW THEM TO FORM A COMPLETE LOOP AROUND YOUR NECK. This is no different than telling a child not to blow in the dog's face (or he could get bitten) but most dog books won't tell you that.

* **Unconsciously establishing undesirable behavioral associations.**
If you've ignored your pet Burmese for the last three months because you've had to put in extra hours at your job and the only time you open its cage is to toss in the rabbit, you are unconsciously conditioning your snake to expect food and therefore to be prepared to strike every time you open the cage. So don't be surprised if after three months without any handling, you open up the cage to pick up your pet and get nailed. Many people establish behaviors associated with

handling prior to picking up a snake. Some use a snake stick and move the forward part of the body and gently stroke the snake before picking a snake up. Others will cover the head with a piece of cloth and gently stroke the back of their snake before picking it up. A lot will depend on the routines that you establish. If your snake is well fed and if you regularly take it out for handling, the snake will not necessarily associate the opening of the door with feeding. So think about the associations you are creating and think snake.
THINK!!

BITES ETC.

The standard defensive behavior of all large constrictors including Burmese pythons is to strike, bite and quickly release. Initially, all hatchling Burmese pythons have a low threshold for defensive behavior (striking out and biting) but within a relatively short period of time and with regular handling, this behavioral propensity in many Burmese pythons will gradually subside. But like people, all Burmese pythons are not created alike. There will be those individuals who remain nervous and restless when handled. Some of those individuals will be unpredictable and will occasionally strike out and bite. There will also be those uptight few who will persist in their nastiness to the point that they will grow into perfectly predictable nippy adults. Besides aggression, most people are bitten by Burmese pythons as a result of poor feeding practices. In most cases, bites can be prevented by adopting better herpetocultural practices The consequences of Burmese python bites will vary in direct relation to size. A bite from a hatchling Burmese will inflict pinpoint punctures and lacerations which will be somewhat painful but of no great or lasting consequence. On the other hand, an adult Burmese python can inflict deep lacerations and multiple puncture wounds with much more serious consequences. Many factors can contribute to the severity of the bite, particularly whether the individual pulls back when the bite is inflicted or the snake pulls back while the teeth remain imbedded in the wounds. Under certain circumstances, a bad bite from an adult Burmese python can require stitches and result in scars. Bites by large pythons also tend to readily become infected. There are many parallels to dogs with this issue. A gentle, good dispositioned Burmese is very unlikely to bite except in cases involving bad feeding practices or other special circumstances. On the other hand nasty or uptight Burmese are more likely to bite but these can be so predictably nasty that necessary precautions can be taken whenever they are handled. The worst cases involving bites are often associated with bad feeding practices which result in a bite followed by constriction i.e., the dummy who dangled a prekilled rabbit by the scruff of the neck in front of his large Burmese to incite it to strike and ended up with 14 feet of python holding on with God knows how many teeth imbedded in his hand, retaining its hold and constricting more and more as the "prey" just kept on moving. With sound herpetocultural practices, bites by Burmese pythons can easily be prevented.

DEALING WITH PROBLEMS INVOLVING CONSTRICTION

Problems involving constriction usually result either from feeding two snakes in the same cage (one constricts the other while both are trying to feed on the same prey item) or the very rare circumstances where a human is involved.

In the first case, the easy solution is to prevent it. Never feed two large snakes together in the same cage. The result can be skin and eye injuries, broken ribs and damage to internal organ.

If faced with this problem and assuming that you were a responsible herpetoculturist and had a friend nearby when the snakes involved were over eight feet long, each person should simply each grab a snake behind the head and try to get the most easily removed one to release its grip. Unwind at least one of them, keeping a hold behind the head, and place it in a separate cage. Next time, don't feed them in the same cage.

In the very rare case of a human or part of a human (an arm is often involved) constricted by a snake the procedure is the same but speed may be critical. If the head is placed such that it can't be made to easily release it's grip, then unwind by the tail end. You can deal with the head later.

WATCH THAT TAIL

Some Burmese are so nasty that handling them requires either the use of a snake stick and holding the tail or, in cases where treatment might be necessary grabbing the snake behind the head and holding the rest of the body (a second person should be present with any large snake over eight feet when performing this procedure). Under these circumstances, nasty or nervous Burmese have a knack for expelling copious amounts of urine and foul-smelling musk. Sometimes they may also defecate. So watch that tail and hold it in such a way that you don't get " sprayed". The end result could be smeared and smelly clothes that will require changing. Furthermore you will stink and will need to take a shower. So beware of that tail.

Notes on Other Large Pythons

INDIAN PYTHON, *Python molurus molurus*

This species has also been called by some the Asiatic rock python. It's most obvious distinguishing feature is the attractive light coloration. Another feature is that the lance shaped mark on top of the head is usually distinct only posteriorly. If uncertain whether you have a pure Indian or an Indian x Burmese hybrid, a useful character involves the scalation beneath the eyes. In pure Indians the 6th or 7th labial will usually reach the edge of the eye while in Burmese, the labials are separated from the eye by subocular scales.

Distribution: Western Pakistan, Nepal, India.

Protection: Because the U.S. listed it as endangered under the Endangered Species Act, this species cannot be sold or transported between states without a special permit from the U.S. Fish and Wildlife department. An unfortunate consequence of this regulation has been a trend towards hybridizing Indian with Burmese pythons to avoid the hassles of red tape etc.

Temperament: While many authors have raved about the docile personality of Indian pythons, in the author's experience, Burmese pythons as a whole are more docile than most of the Indian pythons currently offered in the trade.

Maintenance: Similar to Burmese pythons.

Breeding: Similar to Burmese pythons but usually breeds at an older age and not as reliably or consistently as Burmese pythons.

SRI LANKAN PYTHON, *P. molurus pimbura (also considered as Python molurus molurus Sri Lanka form)* .

Though the Sri Lankan python is now also considered as just a variety of *Python molurus molurus* (which means that U.S. Fish and Wildlife could now consider it as an Appendix I, E.S.A animal), most herpetoculturists believe this to be a sufficiently distinct form to warrant it's recognition as a separate subspecies but....herpetoculturists are not herpetologists. The Sri Lankan python is nonetheless a markedly different insular form of *Python molurus* characterized by a distinctive high contrast pattern, more prominent eyes, subtle morphological differences and consistently more aggressive temperament that make it unmistakable from the mainland Indian python. Sri Lankan pythons are currently bred by relatively few herpetoculturists. As a rule, they are the least docile of the molurus complex. In fact most of the animals currently bred and offered for sale in the U.S. rank among the nastiest pythons one is likely to encounter. Regular handling from the time they are hatchlings will have relatively little effect on the temperament of these animals. At best, they will grow into consistently unreliable adults. These are attractive animals in their own right but if you are looking for a pet, this would probably not be a very good choice.

Maintenance and breeding: Similar to the Indian python but does not breed as readily.

RETICULATED PYTHON, *Python reticulatus.*
This common giant snake is one of the most beautiful of the large constrictors. As a captive, it presents three major problems, fast growth rate, large size and for many specimens a temperamental personality (read that to mean nippy) by the time they reach sexual maturity. Yet many herpetoculturists consider reticulated pythons a more alert and more intelligent snake than the comparatively "sluggish" Burmese. Many claim that reticulated pythons that are regularly interacted with show signs of individual recognition of their owners. The more complex behaviors of reticulated pythons are best observed when they are maintained in room size enclosures in which the owner literally enters their territory. Careful selection of animals for temperament and frequent interaction is essential if one wants to have a reticulated python that remains tame and trustworthy. This is not a snake for beginners. Most people will not put in the time and money required to maintain these animals in a satisfactory manner. If you want a large docile pet, you're better off with a Burmese python.

Size: *Python reticulatus* is consistently the fastest growing and longest of the large constrictors. Under an optimal feeding regimen, a hatchling can exceed 12 feet in two years. Captive-raised females over 18 feet are not uncommon. There are occasional specimens over twenty feet. The record for this species is 33 feet.

Maintenance: Similar to Burmese except that reticulated pythons should be kept in much larger cages, preferably room-sized cages for adults.

Morphs: Several morphs of this python are recognized in the trade. Some of the most outstanding are the yellow-head forms with a beautiful iridescent golden yellow head and a yellowish sheen to the body. Other forms include "silver retics" with very light silvery grey heads and background coloration and dwarf forms said to originate from Timor. Various color and pattern morphs of reticulated pythons including a type of albino are also occasionally available.

Maintenance: Similar to Burmese pythons but requires larger enclosures.

Breeding: Similar to but less consistent than Burmese pythons. Can breed as early as two years but will often not breed until four years or more. Reticulated pythons do not usually breed every year. Cooling to the mid 70's in early fall is usually sufficient to induce breeding. In captivity, typically breeds in the fall. Close attention must be given to the ambient temperature if maternal incubation is allowed because of the limited ability of reticulated pythons to raise their body temperature. In captivity, eggs incubated at 88-90F require about 90 days to hatch.

AFRICAN ROCK PYTHON, *Python sebae.*
Two subspecies *Python sebae sebae* and *Python sebae natalensis.*

Distribution: Africa south of the Sahara.

Size: Hatchlings average about two feet. Adults typically 11-18 feet. Largest specimens are *Python s. sebae* from West Africa. Record nearly 32 feet.

Longevity: There is a record of an African rock python having lived at the San Diego Zoo for 27 years and 4 months.

Comments: In proportion this snake is more like a reticulated python than a Burmese. In terms of growth and maintenance much of what has been said about reticulated pythons applies here. When raised from hatchlings, some African rock pythons grow into relatively docile adults but many tend to be temperamental and likely to occasionally bite. Imported adults are typically infested with parasites and do not always acclimate well.

Breeding: Seldom bred in the U.S. partially because of relatively little interest by herpetoculturists in this species. Otherwise, breeding similar to Burmese python. Cooling to 75F recommended during pre-breeding conditioning. At a temperature of 88-90F, eggs will hatch in 72 to 76 days.

Source Materials

Frye, F. 1981. Biomedical and Surgical Aspects of Captive Reptile Husbandry. Krieger Pub. Melbourne, FL.

Wagner, E. and D. Richardson. 1989. A safe, practical python facility. Proceedings of the 13th International Symposium on captive propagation and husbandry. pp 111-112.

Wagner, E. 1976. Breeding the Burmese python *Python molurus bivittatus* at Seattle Zoo. Int. Zoo. Yearb. 16: pp83-85

Highly recommended for anyone seriously interested in breeding pythons and boas:

The Reproductive Husbandry of Pythons and Boas
by Richard A. Ross and Gerald Marzec. 1991.

Available through book dealers and specialized reptile stores or from
The Institute for Herpetological Research
P.O. Box 2227, Stanford CA, 94305

Product information
Enclosures:
Neodesha Plastics Inc
Twin Rivers Industrial park
P.O. Box 371
Neodesha, KS 66757

Pig blankets/Fiberglass heating pads:
Osborne Industries
P.O. Box 388
Osborne, KS 67473